Breaking Through as a Professional Massage Therapist

Breaking Through as a Professional Massage Therapist

✦

Uncovering Your Inner Tools For Success

Greg Spindler, LMT, CSET

iUniverse, Inc.
New York Lincoln Shanghai

Breaking Through as a Professional Massage Therapist
Uncovering Your Inner Tools For Success

iUniverse books may be ordered through booksellers or by contacting:

iUniverse
2021 Pine Lake Road, Suite 100
Lincoln, NE 68512
www.iuniverse.com
1-800-Authors (1-800-288-4677)

Because of the dynamic nature of the Internet, any Web addresses or links contained in this book may have changed since publication and may no longer be valid.

ISBN: 978-0-595-47946-7 (pbk)
ISBN: 978-0-595-60527-9 (ebk)

Printed in the United States of America

Second Edition

For contact information, please visit www.gregspindler.com.

Contents

Foreword. ix

Part I   *Discover and Develop Your Inner Self*

CHAPTER 1   Who You Are 3

CHAPTER 2   What You Are 9

CHAPTER 3   When You Are. 17

CHAPTER 4   Where You Are 22

CHAPTER 5   Why You Are. 27

CHAPTER 6   How You Are As a Therapist 35

Part II   *A Healthy Practice and a Healthy You*

CHAPTER 7   Get Clients Fast, Without Spending a Lot of
                Money. 43

CHAPTER 8   Marketing Your Business Using Ads, Flyers,
                Brochures and Articles. 49

CHAPTER 9   Wellness, Simplified 53

About the Author 61

Foreword

Over the years that I have been practicing massage therapy, I have noticed a trend among therapists, one that prevents them from reaching their fullest potential not only in their businesses and with their clients, but also personally. They lose enthusiasm and burn out. It is sad to think that someone would commit to the time and financial expense of an education, only to allow their dream to go unfulfilled. For most, the dream I am speaking of is to help others while supporting themselves and creating a decent living. Even though recipients of massage have doubled in the past ten years, many people still do not realize the value of massage therapy and its positive effects on health and wellness. My purpose for writing this book is to help therapists become the best they can be quickly and stay in the business so that the profession can be further recognized as a valuable tool for wellness.

Although it is one of the oldest healing therapies, massage therapy is still virtually unrecognized by many within the field of modern medicine. We, as therapists, have the opportunity to help those in need of our services with the pure and simple language of touch. The energy exchange from one to another has the ability to accomplish so much. The power of intention goes farther than scientific research can prove. With awareness now emerging that prescription drugs, surgeries, and other forms of traditional western medicine should actually be last resorts, this industry will continue to gain recognition. There is plenty of room for more gifted, talented, and trained therapists to educate and work with people in need of the wide variety of modalities that are offered.

For whatever reason, the lifespan of the average therapist is quite short. Do they wear out? Do they have bad business practices? Do they just rub people the wrong way (no pun intended)? Perhaps it is simply that they have not found their special niche within the business, one that would give them a true sense of purpose. None of these reasons are good for the profession; so I am writing this book as a manual to help you, the therapist, become successful in your practice. You might even find that the information I share will transcend into other areas of your life.

The chapters in this book will give you the two-part basics on how to discover your potential as a great therapist. First, I will explain how to develop your inner-self in order to help you find your niche. Secondly, I will provide some proven mastery techniques to help you reach your goals. The two must work together in order to be successful. Unfortunately, most people do not understand how the two interact to create the momentum necessary for a strong massage therapy business.

This book does not preach about networking, marketing, or business tactics for success, although these topics are addressed briefly. Rather, it is about bringing out the best in you each day, week, month, and year to come. True success starts from within. In my opinion, you must develop yourself in order to experience the desired results in the outside world. Together, we will attempt to identify the issues that could be holding you back, even if just a little. When applied, the simple tools and ideas that I explain will open new avenues for success.

The obvious "nuts and bolts" of massage therapy is that one must first have clients. How you acquire and retain clients is determined by the consistency of your actions throughout your career. It is also based on the answers to six basic questions: who you are, what you are, where you are, when you are in your career, why you are in the profession, and how you are. Wow, that's a lot to think about. I will explain these throughout the book. The answers to these questions differ from individual to individual, and they absolutely determine the best way to build your client list.

There are many ways to get clients, and no matter what method you use, the key ingredient is a genuine understanding of why each one came to you. What was it that you did right to get that client? If you do this successfully and sincerely, the client will likely choose to spread the word about your services, i.e. REFERRALS! From a business perspective, there are three basic reasons some individuals do not get a massage or bodywork. These are money, time, and fear (or lack of trust). If you have one client who meets these three criteria (money, time, and trust), it stands to reason that he/she knows others who will also.

I will focus more on these three criteria later; however, let's take a brief look at them. When a client pays for your services, money is exchanged for your time. Yes, of course, but also NO! In the client's eyes, it is viewed as an exchange of their precious time. Often, a client might fear that bodywork is not worth the time given the other demands on their lives. They are putting trust in you that it is worth their time (and money) and they rightfully expect positive results from the treatment. There must be client satisfaction for you to be successful. For this to happen, it is imperative that you begin with a unique purpose that stands out from the rest. I will address this and other issues throughout the book.

People exchange time and money for two things in life: PAIN and PLEA-SURE. It is a cycle that goes around and around, over and over again. People want to be released from pain in order to have, or be able to create, more pleasure. When pleasure is excessive (out of balance), pain is sent in to stop the pleasure cycle. So as therapists, we are in a very good position, and it is up to us to make it happen. It takes a lot of hard work, but I will explain how you can make it a little easier. You must be open to new self-understandings and apply what you learn. It took me several years to realize that it is not only about the work you do, but also the work that you must do on yourself.

This book is intended for those who truly desire success in their lives. What you get out of it is based on the actions you take. There might be some parts that are shocking to you, or perhaps they "hit home" a little bit. Do not take it personally, but do take it seriously. Examine yourself honestly and note your responses at the end of each chapter. If some of your responses are, "Oh, I know that," but your actions do not reflect it, then where lies the problem? If you find any of the information or the exercises I present in this book to be "hokey" or a waste of time, then you are simply not ready for success at this time in your life. You must be open to change and new ways of thinking. Success will evade you until you are ready to work on yourself.

Enjoy the reading.

PART I

Discover and Develop Your Inner Self

1

Who You Are

It is not often that you hear of someone entering the massage therapy business as their very first profession. Most newcomers have spent some years in other professions or jobs and are still adjusting to life's direction. Our paths sometimes take turns that are unexpected and cannot be predicted. This swaying path of life experiences helps you become WHO YOU ARE!

Take a moment to go back in time. Note what was going on in your life and chart the events on a timeline. Note: If you are currently very young, your timeline cannot go far into the past. In this case, label your scale in one-year increments instead of five-year increments as I have in this example. This will allow more memories to return to you.

Example:

Year … What happened_____

2005_____

2000_____

1995_____

1990_____

1985_____

1980_____

1975_____

1970_____

Record the events in your good years, bad years, sluggish years, and meaningful years. You might be surprised by the cycles and patterns that you discover. Like the stock market, these are cyclical changes that follow your achievements, accelerations, and downturns. Your timeline will likely reveal patterns during successful periods, magical moments, and downward trends or slumps. Reflect on what you were doing right during the positive cycles and what was happening during the negatives. You might even find yourself returning to some forgotten events that you did not fully address years ago. This is your unfinished business that requires closure. Some projects just seem to stay with us subconsciously. The experiences of your past help guide your decision-making. What you have dealt with, overcome, and/or accomplished in your life all contribute to the person you are today.

Many therapists leave the profession very early on for a variety of reasons such as physical burnout, mental fatigue, and/or lack of work in order to support themselves. When these therapists entered the industry, one must wonder if they had ever asked themselves, "Who am I, and how can this relate to being a therapist?" This is so critical for a successful business in the modern-day world.

Longevity starts on the inside, causing the results in the outside world. These results are reflections of the strong foundation of your inner intentions put into action. The key is to reduce the occurrence of downward cycles. My goal here is to help you recognize the events that lead to these downturns so that you are able to eliminate or reduce them. Being in a rut or "funk" can destroy your confidence, making positive results difficult to achieve.

The old saying, "you can't give what you don't got," is a classic example of what I am talking about. It defines, in the truest sense, exactly what you are able to give to another person (your client). Have you ever noticed how you can really relate to and connect with certain people? Without a word spoken, something you both have in common acts as an underlying energy force, bringing the two of you closer. It is an energy exchange and many medical professionals are baffled by the results that some of our clients experience as a result of it. For some, this ability to connect with others is their niche to acquire clients, and it leads to even more clients just like them through word-of-mouth referrals.

Niches can come from our past because we have been "schooled in the real world" by them. You may have lived it, seen it, tasted it, felt it, did it, and heard it. It is embedded in you, and it all can be exposed or accessed to develop your passion. Where there is passion, there is also focus, followed by actions, which breed success.

Your clients can pick up on this passion and welcome you as their therapist. In other words, do not attempt to be someone or something that you cannot be in your truest form. Some have coined this as your "authentic self." If you are not "real," your clients can detect it by the energy exchange on your first meeting. Without that security blanket of energy, your client will not return. You cannot fake it.

Stick to the truth and be who you really are. This will keep you on course for success. Those therapists who think that every person in the world should come to them for massage will find trouble at some point. In most cases, this occurs sooner rather than later. They end up overworking themselves, often by undercutting the average cost per hour in the market where they work. Commonly, this is the therapist who works for a clinic that overloads their therapists beyond their physical capabilities. For some, the result is mental exhaustion as they try to become an "all around therapist" rather than specializing and becoming a master of a certain modality. Their clients only experience superficial results and the therapist does not get enough work to pay the bills. I like to call this hop-scotching through the industry. You pick up minimal amounts of education to get started but do not follow through with good continuing education and applied experience so that the public sees you as an expert. A therapist must have direction and the public needs to know that you are good at what you do in order to get paid the best. In my opinion, therapists should never think that they have the right type of treatment for everyone. Your clientele needs to select you as a therapist. Not everyone can be your client and you must remember that you do not own your clients.

Over time, we can become attached to some clients as we develop relationships with them. If and when they decide that it is time to break off to explore other treatment options (which they have the right to do), they should be applauded for doing so. I have seen therapists become resentful when clients "ditch them." Therapists should not rely on certain clients to be their revenue sources forever. This dependency is not fair and is certainly not healthy for either party. When such a bond is formed, a sudden breakaway can be toxic to one or both, mentally as well as physically.

The healthy client-therapist relationship should be mutually positive. I find that it is best to start off by setting goals with them. Vocalize your intentions, i.e. to help them be pain free, improve their quality of life, etc. Make it clear that they do not have to rely on or depend on you forever. This gives clients control of their healing and builds their respect for you and your integrity. In my opinion, holding a client for financial gain is a form of captivity and is dishonest.

So, how do you discover who you truly are and find your niche? Well, you just have to think back. I suggest starting with more current history. Write down what you have done, what you have seen, what has happened to you, and work your way back through different stages of your life. It often helps to put events in categories. Let me give my own example:

• Traumatic Injuries or Incidents:

1.   Ruptured disc in lumbar, needed surgery

2.   Motorcycle accident

3.   Bicycle accidents

4.   Repetitive use injuries of plantar fascia, ITB syndrome, and Achilles tendonitis from running

5.   Wore a brace between my legs at the age of 2

• Participation in activities or sports:

1.   Yoga classes

2.   15 years of triathlon training and racing

3.   High school cross-country and track, east coast national competitor

4.   3 years of Karate

5.   10 years in landscape construction business

6.   11 years of playing drums as a hobby

7.   Played youth baseball, football, and basketball

• Certification in USAT coaching
• Certification in Personal Training
• Certified Structural Energetic Therapist and teaching assistant
• Have worked in chiropractic clinic
• Have worked in a spa facility
• Have traveled through parts of Europe
• Have spoken, taught, and demonstrated ergonomics at health fairs for corporate businesses

This list could go on and on into finer details from my memories. Looking at it, can you see all of the potential niches available? I chose to focus on my athletic experience. I have several years of running and involvement in the sport of triathlon. What a niche this has been for me. I could network, run ads, create brochures, and speak about my accomplishments within the sport and how massage therapy relates to it. This has resulted in close bonds with those who schedule appointments with me. During the initial treatment session, I know what questions to ask in order to build a sense of security and a strong relationship. Furthermore, I am in a position to understand their needs. For example, I could ask the athlete about what part of their training phase they are in. Then, "How many weeks out are you from your peak race?" My clients become aware that I know something about the sport in which they are involved. This is key. Successful therapists are able to relate to their clients and convey that they have the knowledge and experience to help them.

In the above example, imagine a therapist who does not have knowledge of the sport. There is no positive energy exchange. During the entire session, the client could be thinking of all the time and money being wasted. A return visit is highly unlikely. Search *who you are* and strengthen your niche(s) to help ensure a thriving therapy practice. The power within us creates passion. Without passion, there can be no success. It is one of the most observable traits among all successful people, no matter what they are doing.

Right now, make a list for yourself.

_____

_____

_____

_____

_____

_____

_____

_____

_____

_____

_____

Now review your list and begin by picking out your strongest experiences. These are usually the ones that you recalled rather easily. They often involve either pain or great achievement. Capitalize on these experiences. They define who you are and help you develop confidence, knowledge, and passion for your work. Next, give some thought to your current clients who seem to fall into similar categories. They are likely to know others just like themselves who can also become your clients. Failure to tap into this source can be just one of the missing links for your success. Now take the list you used to create your timeline and compare it with your life experiences list. Highlight or list all of the positives. These are your achievements and successes, the ones that support you emotionally.

My positive example was in 1996. I was able to qualify for and compete in the Boston Marathon, the Hawaii Ironman, and then in the Atlanta marathon where I was a top ten finisher. This was a break-out year for me. I quit my job, became a therapist, moved to Colorado and started my own business. In 1998, I returned to Tampa, Florida and met my wife, Kami. This was a huge momentum builder for me. My clients were mostly triathlon and running athletes who sought my help because of my experience and knowledge of their sport. It made them feel secure that they were spending their time and money wisely (the biggest fear that prevents people from getting massage therapy). I was uniquely qualified to meet their needs.

You can also turn negative incidents into positives. These "down years" do not generate momentum, but you can transform them into assets nevertheless. For example, I had a rupture in the L-4 area of my spine. Because of my first-hand experience with this condition, I have a unique ability to help others with similar issues. I can market it, engage in continuing education, and specialize in it. Part of my health learning series within my Structural Energetic Therapy practice is called *Life after Back Surgery*.

I often hear people say that they have trouble finding their niche. They claim that they have not had any events or experiences from which they can pull information. Break out a photo album, a yearbook, or call old friends if you need to. Stir up the past. In my S.U.C.C.E.S.S. seminars, we work on this together and I show you that there are more available to you than you realize. Life is made up of experiences. Every day is a new experience born within you to expand upon. So take advantage of what is given to you each day. This lays the groundwork for the foundation of your massage practice.

Chapter One Notes:

2

What You Are

After doing the necessary work to learn *who* you are, it is time to determine *what you are*. Are you a procrastinator, a workaholic, organized, unorganized? Are you a leader or follower? Do you complete things or just get things done halfway and stop? Look again at your timeline in the last chapter and focus on evidence of the habits that you have formed over your life.

Look around at your workplace and your home. What do you see? Is there clutter? These are all reflections of your current habits and make up a part of what you are. What do you think might happen if you were just a little bit better organized, you worked smarter not harder, and you removed the clutter? Some of you might feel somewhat skeptical and that is okay. But remember, to make positive changes in your life, you must be open to thoroughly investigating other possibilities *before* you choose to dismiss them.

Organize the Clutter

I feel I need to emphasize what clutter really is since it has the power to define what you are (or at least part of you). A cluttered environment = a mind cluttered with thoughts and ideas. In the massage business, it can mean cluttered techniques: lack of organization, focus, or specialization. It is just a little of this, a little of that. This will certainly be apparent in the quality of your work. Your goals will lack direction, your intentions will not be as strong, and your clients will experience declining results from your treatments.

For instance, you might forget certain protocols while treating your clients or begin to develop bad habits such as failing to return calls promptly, arriving late for appointments, dressing inappropriately for work, and other poor business practices. Some therapists might allow their bills to accumulate (this wreaks havoc on one's finances and can lead to an extremely stressful situation). Inevitably, attention to clients will not be 100% and results will surely be minimal. This equates to minimal pay and a diminishing client list.

Clutter also includes taking on more clients than you can handle, not only physically, but mentally as well. Certain choices you make, such as overbooking, result in spreading yourself too thin. However, many therapists do not realize that they make the same mistake when they take on a client list that is too broad. It is important to specialize in order to avoid the "all around therapist syndrome." Too many massage therapists "suffer" with this "condition." They want to have everyone as a client.

Do not kid yourself by believing that you can effectively treat everyone. In this case, more is definitely not better. This scenario will ultimately compromise treatment quality and is certainly not a good way to retain clients or to gain new ones. Focus on the big picture and your long-term goals for success. Do not overload yourself! The Workaholic is someone who is out of balance. They do not schedule in the other aspects of life that create balance. True, workaholics usually make a lot of money. But in the massage therapy business, doing too much hands-on work for your physical capabilities means you will not last. You will work so much that you drain your body of the positive energy forces that are essential to share with others. Ultimately, this will reflect in your work.

Organization is vital. Get rid of clutter in your workplace and at home. You rarely find it in a successful environment. I suggest you take it slowly, a bit at a time. Real change does not happen overnight. Start by scheduling your activities in a daily planner to establish better habits for yourself. I am sure you have heard this before, but "don't knock it 'til you try it" consistently. You will notice that planning and organization will, indeed, help you accomplish your goals. Your business will prosper from it.

I have found that all areas of my life benefit when I improve my organization. It helps to begin by surveying your current habits in the workplace. Respond to the following questions on a scale from one to ten (and be honest!).

1. Did you get there on time?

2. Is the desk clean? Can you see the surface? (Or are there stacks of clutter?)

3. Is the massage table clean and ready for your next client? (Or does it have your last client's sheets from the previous day's work on it?)

4. Are the intake forms readily accessible and SOAP reports put away?

5. Are files orderly? Are the books in bookcases standing upright?

6. Is the carpet or floor clean? Are wastebaskets emptied or overflowing?

7. Are bathrooms clean and ready for clients?

8. Is your schedule book open to the correct day?

9. Are there any odors from food coming from the break room?

10. Is the entrance to the building inviting?

These are just a few issues that could apply to you. Use this checklist consistently to grade yourself and improve your habits. It can be helpful to visit other "successful" massage therapy offices. You will likely find that their organizational standards are high. You might also consider exchanging services with others, including other therapists, to get some candid feedback from them.

The next time you do a massage treatment, survey yourself:

1. Is there structure to what you are doing?

2. Are you rushing through certain parts of the treatment?

3. If you play music, does it last the entire session? Is it your choice or your client's choice?

4. Did you run out of lotion and have to refill the container?

5. Are there any potential interruptions such as telephones ringing or your need for restroom breaks?

6. Are your face cradles, pillows, and bolsters readily available?

7. At the end of the session, can you honestly say that it went well?

I once practiced massage therapy in a ski resort. Of course, all of the therapists wanted work in order to pay their bills. It was that feast or famine concept. Some weeks were very hectic and busy. We were overbooked and delivering poor quality due to exhaustion. This over-scheduling by management led to therapists dropping out, thus increasing the workload for those of us who remained. Management was truly only concerned about surviving with enough therapists for each season, not the health of the therapists and the quality of service. I cannot express enough how important it is to schedule in breaks and vacations with everything you do. Create a balance. Without balance, we are lopsided and overloaded on one side. Our bodies are like wheels. To roll along smoothly, they need balance. Overloading or adding weight to one side wears the wheel down. Sooner or later, it will break down. We too, will succumb to illness or injury without proper balance.

Here is an example of how you can schedule your day to include appropriate breaks:

9:00 A.M.—1st client
10:30 A.M.—2nd client
12:00 P.M.—lunch break
1:00 P.M.—3rd client
2:30 P.M.—4th client
4:00 P.M.—5th client
5:30 P.M.—close office

This schedule allows you to spend up to 90 minutes with each client. Keep in mind, 5 clients at 60-90 minutes each is a very physically demanding day. Although you might be tempted to add one or two more clients, your body requires rest. Demanding too much of it will affect your longevity in this profession. As I mentioned before, work smarter, not harder. Hone in on a specialized skill so that clients are willing to pay a premium rate for your time and expertise. This will result in a lucrative business with staying power.

Follow-Through

Are you someone who is unorganized or doesn't complete things? Completing tasks is the focus here. Your success depends on it. Time after time we can start an idea or project and never finish it. You may have recognized this within a downward trend on your timeline. Perhaps you had too many projects on the list and not enough time to pay them adequate attention. No matter what it is that you begin and do not finish, it carries on to the next project or task because it is HABIT FORMING and, believe it or not, you are PROGRAMMING YOUR-SELF. How sad is that? I have fallen short on many projects in my lifetime. Why? I don't know. Perhaps you can relate. I would literally spend hours planning things, making outlines, and dreaming of the end results. Some of the projects I would start and then get distracted by some negative feedback from others or even within myself when it became challenging. I would get frustrated and scrap the idea.

Be careful who you listen to, including yourself. When someone offers advice, make sure you are receiving it from someone who has experience and knowledge in the area. Some people are so negative and stuck in their own box of thinking that they will try to keep you with them for their own comfort. Others just like to sound like an authority on all matters, even when they are actually clueless. My theory is if one person can do it, then all people can do it. Just maybe, you could be the first to do it. I have given up on ideas only to see, a year later, someone else do something very similar to the project I had started and then given up on, all because I listened to the negative chatter within myself or from others. I was ready to beat myself up. Once I made up my mind not to fall short anymore, I began to check off accomplishments towards my goals. It is like a snowball effect. Hard tasks became easy once I made the decision to follow through.

If any of this sounds familiar, it is time to change. Decide to finish ALL things you start. I am not saying that you need to be a perfectionist, but be an "A" player in follow-through. "A's" get paid the best. This is true in all areas of life such as professional athletics, heads of businesses, and creators of products or merchandise. In each case, the best reap the most compensation and opportunities. By accepting "C" grades, you are settling to be poor, both financially and in your opportunities for success. It is a habit, a conditioned zone. If you want more success for yourself, raise your game level.

Leaders and Followers

What you are is not only determined by your organizational skills, it also depends on whether you are a leader or a follower. One is not necessarily better than the other, but the answer will help you learn more about yourself. While observing others in all sorts of fields, sports, classes, etcetera, I have noticed that there always seem to be individuals who stand out. These people seem to rise to the occasion no matter what the task. They engage themselves in new adventures. They get involved and volunteer. They somehow create time to help others and have the natural ability to lead. Even if you tend to be a follower, it is important to learn to pick up on some of these traits. Why? It is because opportunities always seem to fall on the laps of these types. Is it luck? No. It is the law of the universe. The goals that they are setting lead to opportunities which they seize. A strong desire to achieve, coupled with preparation, is a winning combination. This is the power of intention.

You may have heard that the definition of insanity is doing the same things over and over in your life and expecting different results. Make a positive change, even a small change. If you want different results, you need different daily, weekly, and annual tasks, ideas and thoughts put into action. Too many people rely on that typical "9 to 5" routine and then expect something different. To me, this sounds like living within a herd of cows. You are stuck in the middle and getting pushed around without having a say as to what to do. This is "following the crowd" in the worst sense.

I remember playing sports and schoolyard games during my childhood. It seemed that I was always picked to be the captain, i.e. the leader. It is a trait I think I received by watching my father as a motivated leader within his teaching profession. After a while, it just became automatic for me to volunteer to lead. Becoming a leader is quite a niche to have. It absolutely does not make a person any better than anyone else; but it does give you a certain level of credibility. Credibility, as we know, attracts a lot of things and one of them is financial gain through a larger client list. It creates exposure. You will more likely be noticed by others, both within your field and by potential clients.

Now, let me address the advantages of being a follower. These folks are often open, teachable, and in the perfect position to learn from those whom they admire. Learning from others has countless benefits as long as you choose carefully who you emulate. But the question is, how long should one listen, learn, and wait before taking action? However vague it might sound, the answer is *not too long*. One must practice what one has learned. Without the doing, learning is not complete and nothing will ever happen. Furthermore, whatever you heard and observed from your mentor will not be retained. We have to practice and apply what we've learned, particularly in this profession, in order to be good at what we do.

Conquering Fear

Timing is everything for most of us. We change when we are willing to stretch comfort ranges and conquer that which holds us back. For just about everyone, this thing I'm speaking of is FEAR. No matter how different two people may be, fear is a factor that can easily affect both of them for it takes many different forms for different reasons. You might have a fear of rejection, a fear of loss, or a fear of failure. Believe it or not, many people actually have a fear of success and do not even realize it. They unknowingly do things to sabotage their own success. You might remember my previous discussion regarding how experiences shape our lives and define *who* we are. These same experiences also play a crucial role in *what* we are and the steps we take, both consciously and subconsciously.

It is necessary to knock on the door of your fears in order to raise yourself and your business to the next level. This might require more self-examination. To stay within the zone in which you are comfortable, which is the "C" player in you, is to continue to support your current level. You must stretch yourself more. Not all at once, but little by little so that it is an enjoyable process. For example, there was a time during my career when I felt satisfied with my income level within my practice. However, I wanted more out of my practice for my clients. I wanted more knowledge so that they would experience better results. This meant I had to be open to changing (improving) some of my techniques and, in turn, possibly losing some clients who were accustomed to my "old" methods. Not only did I have to face my fears of changing my business practices, but also the fears of changing my clients' belief systems. I had to prepare myself for their fears of experiencing something different. I took a leap a faith and so did most of my clients. We are all happier and better as a result.

Your Inspiration

What you are also results from that which inspires you. Your inspiration might come from certain people. Mentors, teachers, and other professionals can provide a lift to our spirits and ignite us. I have experienced great opportunities largely because of people who have been in the profession longer than I have. I am honored by their willingness to share their knowledge with me. For example, a true friend in the wellness business shared some insights with me that have stimulated my desire to write this book and to work on my own health issues.

Magical moments can also inspire us, such as the births of my two boys. Even weather can inspire with its invigorating pleasant temperatures or sunrises and sunsets with spectacular colors. What inspires you might change frequently or can endure a lifetime. What motivates you to get out of bed in the morning? As therapists, we tend to get caught up in taking care of others. It is a gift that we can present to others. Our clients inspire us, don't they? But who or what else does? During our lives we meet people who just happen to show up to help or assist us at just the right time, some for short durations and others for longer relationships. They might not give us hands-on help directly, but rather indirectly through inspiration. We are renewed with enthusiasm to get something done or to achieve something. This is part of your support system, a survival mechanism so to speak. I encourage you to try to recognize these inspiring events or people. It could result in accomplishing something that you did not know you had the ability to do.

For me, this book is the ultimate example of an unexpected accomplishment. In high school, I was told that I could not write. I believed that teacher. After all, she was supposed to be the expert on the subject. As a result, I had no further interest in writing at that time. There was no passion or desire behind it. But later in my life, I met someone who stimulated me enough to write something. Finally, I was inspired with a passion to write and the ability just seemed to come about without much effort. As a result, I created another niche for myself within the marketplace to give me further credibility. Being a published author increases public awareness of my services. As you can see, passion and desire are two elements to success that go hand-in-hand.

These are just a few examples of how to discover *what you are*. Your current actions yield your current results and are, therefore, what you need to address. Take some time now to examine yourself honestly so that you can make corrections. The more you adjust the actions that are holding you back, the more successful you will become.

Chapter Two Notes:

3

When You Are

To be an effective massage therapist, you must work at your best at all times. This is quite a challenge. When are you at your best? More specifically, when are you at your best for your clients? For most, it is when you are at peace, happy, and naturally energized. In this state, therapists can produce a power from within which results in optimal healthcare for the client. A thriving business becomes inevitable. Sounds easy, doesn't it? However, we must understand that therapists are people too. We go through emotions just like anyone else: happiness, sadness, anger, love, and fear issues each day of our lives. We can become distracted from the task that is right in front of us. This does not help when trying to run a business.

Your State of Mind

In the wrong frame of mind, you could miss an opportunity when it presents itself. How many times have you heard the saying "being in the right place at the right time"? This adage applies to your mental and emotional states as well. Coming across as a person who is depressed, distracted, frustrated with the current issue of the day, or lacking energy can all sabotage the relationships that you have with your clients. Each of our thoughts, feelings, and beliefs can temporarily affect our performance as a therapist. Remember, they (the clients) rightfully expect us to be happy, understanding, supportive, and energized for them during their appointment. They are looking for solutions. You are best able to provide this when you are at your best.

You may have been told by some clients that you are their mental health counselor as well as their massage therapist. As a result, when the client says something that triggers you, you might feel obligated to make it your problem too, something that directly affects your mind-processing. Or, you take some comment personally and become worried about disapproval from others just because you have a different opinion. This can pull you down, make you angry and out of focus, and keep you down, even while you work on others. You will not feel at peace, happiness will be shut down, and your energy level will become sluggish or will fluctuate. This temporary "out-of-performance" mode can wreck your business or simply create a plateau that prevents your business from taking off.

It can also weaken you physically. You can use kinesiology testing to confirm this. Ask a friend to help you. Hold your right arm straight out in front of you while your friend tests your strength by pushing down on your arm and you resist their downward pressure. Then repeat this process while the friend tells you how much he/she dislikes you. (Note: The person does not really have to dislike you. They only need to tell you so when testing your arm strength.) You will see that your arm goes weak. Negativity leads to weakness. As therapists, it is vital that we keep ourselves at full strength, not only for ourselves, but also for our clients.

Many therapists who decided to leave the profession might have had trouble dealing with the negative energy they absorbed from their clients. This emotional over-stimulation can be very taxing. Having to deal with one's own issues and then clients' issues on a daily basis, it's no wonder that stress pushes so many therapists out of the field. It can become just too much to handle. When we are not able to let that negativity pass through us, it can cause us to dislike ourselves and disturb the process of becoming a quality therapist. Imagine all of the problems you could potentially take on during a single week in a full-time massage practice. This is very toxic to the human body. Stressful emotions build acidic cells in the body, forcing it to work on overload in order to correct. It weakens the performance of the mind-to-body relationship. Over time, this can bring on illness and encourage poor habits and decision-making.

We all have clients who have robbed us of energy. They are like energy vampires, sinking with a bite that is so disturbing that you just want to scream. It's easy to get stuck dealing with one client's troubles all day. It is as though only part of you shows up for the next client—not good for your health and not fair to your other paying clients. It is necessary to "clear yourself" when you feel that you have absorbed your clients' issues. I like to clear myself after each client while washing up following each session. Simple daily breathing exercises like yoga or meditation can release negativity and tension. Try a mind exercise whereby you go through the major muscle groups of your body, telling them to relax. This can be followed by going through your five senses: taste, smell, touch, hearing, and sight, cleansing each one with your mind. Erase and let go of the troubled thoughts and welcome the positive, supportive ones. Give yourself a few minutes to regain your center so that you can be at 100% for your next client. To prevent problems, begin each day by saying, "I will not take on my clients' problems today." This will put up a barrier or channel that allows those undesirable issues to pass right through you.

To maintain this supportive state, I have props in my office. These props are things that you display in your work environment that uplift you. For example, I use pictures of my wife and kids that I can glance at anytime from the table. Looking at them reminds me of my purpose and provides my enthusiasm for life because they are what is most important to me. I also have a picture of myself crossing the finish line of my most successful Ironman competition. For me, this represents my ability to overcome physical challenges. Also, a large portrait of a soothing waterfall in the mountains of Colorado taken by my mother reflects the peacefulness of nature and how water soothes and nurtures the environment in which we live. It can ease angered thoughts that lead to tension. A tense therapist cannot relieve the tension within a client. It is a law of science: two likes cannot bring change. During sessions, some clients ask me about the photographs of my family that I have on display. It seems as though they provide those clients with a similar positive energy.

Remember that our bodies process everything that we smell, touch, hear, and see. The body actually mirrors mental activity. This can cause postural changes, trigger muscle spasms, relax tensions, and even alleviate headaches. Try an exercise going through each one of these senses. Notice your body's changes with various stimuli. This is a great awareness exercise. For smell, use different aromas, both good and bad. Touch a variety of hot and cold objects, coarse and smooth surfaces, wet and dry, soft and hard, and so on. Listen to loud noises versus a whisper, foul language versus polite words, and a variety of musical instruments. For sight, look at different colors, sunsets and sunrises, darkness versus very bright light. Be aware of how even your pulse can change!

Inspirational audios can also be helpful. I like to listen to motivational cd's and music on my way to work. To the extent that these can help, listening to negative things will further trouble you. Therefore, it is wise to try to avoid too much media news. It is unfortunate that 90% of news today is negative or bad news. Talk about a downer. Do what you can to surround yourself with positive things to look at and listen to, including the people in your life. They can bring you out of "a funk" and keep you in a clear, attentive framework.

Try to keep this formula in mind:

positive thoughts = positive feelings = positive actions
= positive results

Timing

All of us have internal clocks. Our bodies have numerous detailed jobs to do in order to take care of us. Learn about your internal system. You may notice that there are certain times of the day when you are sluggish, tired, and can't work well. Try to discover the reason for this by understanding what your body does 24/7. In most cases, the solution lies within your diet and wellness plan. It always amazes me when therapists make the excuse that they do not have time to eat right and exercise just a little bit each day, yet they do have time to feel bad and work like crap! Those who own this particular argument do not realize how time-consuming this attitude is. It snowballs into a host of other problems that, I guarantee, they do not have time for. You must take responsibility for your health if you want to be taken seriously as a healthcare professional. Do not jeopardize your business. Recognize that if you do not solve the problem and choose to work at this sluggish time, you may be ripping off your clients. It only makes sense not to schedule work at that time. This will help ensure that you are productive and at your best as much as possible.

Success comes with great difficulty to those who resist change or avoid facing their fears. When you are willing to challenge yourself and do things you've never done before, you break out of your comfort zone. Try not to resist change. Look at your surroundings. Haven't they changed over the years? The earth has, your neighborhood has, and your body has. So why not your inner self? Some people do not realize that they are even resistant to themselves. We all have some bad habits, the things that we do over and over that achieve the same negative results. Try to identify them and recognize the things that block you from the solutions. They can often seem undetectable. Start by making a small change or improvement somewhere in your daily routine. Watch how it turns other things into better actions. The mind will begin to want to be stretched, expanded, and developed on a continuing basis. Learning, practicing, and correcting your mistakes or failures seems to become enjoyable rather than a burden.

This leads to an expansion of your money-making opportunities and it is the best way to improve. You educate yourself via your experiences and invest in yourself! From there, you develop new niches in the market. People often procrastinate and make the excuse that they will begin once they have everything in line. Or, they're waiting until they have enough capital/money to take that important class or start marketing. These are all fear-based thoughts. It took me a while to learn this and admit it to myself. I needed to think outside of my security box. So, when will everything be in line? There is always something that keeps the inline part crooked all the time, doesn't it? The right time never really presents itself. So, it just tells you that you must have faith in yourself and do some things outside of your comfort zone in order to expand your business and self-growth opportunities.

Have you ever noticed that you are capable of accomplishing tasks, even those outside of your comfort zone, when your back is against the wall? In my case, I had and still have a fear of speaking in front of others. A few years ago, I was asked to speak at a club meeting for runners. I never thought in a million years I would be involved in public speaking. In high school, speech class was terrifying. Nevertheless, I confronted my fears, accepted the invitation, and spoke to the group. A lot stemmed from that day. I gained new clients, I was invited to speak at other companies, and I bartered talks for membership fees. I added a niche to the market for financial gain. None of this would have happened had I not confronted my fears on that single day. When we grow on the inside, the growth and opportunities outside of us grow too. Never forget, if you keep doing the same things over and over, then you will get the same results over and over.

Chapter Three Notes:

4

Where You Are

Where you are today as a massage therapist affects where you are going in the profession. Try to visualize where you are right now in the industry. Are you happy, secure, and satisfied with what you see? Can you really tell clearly where you are? It is very common to be unable to do this. We are caught in the rat race of everyday life and our habits. And God forbid if they are broken! It can seem like the end of the world if we stray from our routines. But really, look inside and out in terms of where you are as a professional. Since it can be difficult to see the truth about ourselves, it might be helpful to ask for help from someone who can give you feedback about yourself. Make sure that this person knows you well and can be candid about you and your present life direction.

Look at Yourself Objectively

Before you even begin, understand that you are not 100% right all the time. Do not take feedback personally or it will work against you. Be willing to accept someone else's view in order to get the benefits. Besides, how can you possibly grow if you are not willing to listen? If you think you know everything, you are simply unable to improve upon yourself.

Once you begin the process and develop some clarity about where you are, ask yourself some questions. Do you see balance in your life and/or work? Are you overloaded in any one area? Are you doing the same things over and over yet expecting different results? Balance is what we must maintain or strive for in order to have equal energy in all parts of our lives.

If you feel fulfilled and completely satisfied with where you are now and can stay there contentedly for the rest of your professional career, then this chapter is not for you. But keep in mind that, sooner or later, settling could turn into mediocrity which leads to medium pay, medium life, and medium success. This defines the "C" player that I mentioned earlier; one who chooses to just go through the motions everyday and, in turn, always gets the same results.

Now, take the time to look ahead to the therapist you would like to be in 5 years, 10 years, or more. There is no way to predict the future or to determine what will happen along the way, but you can achieve a lot to keep your boat afloat and moving forward instead of sinking.

Close your eyes. Where do you see yourself? If you come up empty, ask yourself where you are currently going in the profession. This picture that you paint for yourself is by no means set in stone. We live in a world that is constantly evolving. That's okay. But what you are seeing is what you really want if there were no obstacles in your career path. It is the raw you and it is your first step in the right direction. You have to know what you want in order to get to where you want to be.

It is now time to think about what it will take to get there. These are the baby steps, obstacles, and learning experiences that are involved in blazing the trail to your goals. They are all going to have to be new or altered from your past strategies if you want to make change happen. It might sound easy but, for most, it can be one of the most difficult elements of change. It might even be scary since it requires a change in routine. It certainly was for me. You must discard past conditioning and stretch outside of your comfort zone.

One of the best ways to begin meeting your goals is to take another look at yourself, but this time you will focus on some history. Study your work patterns and the way you invest your time. This is your engraved evolution and it might be painful to face head-on. I went through this and recognized some disturbing patterns. I realized that I consistently came up short in fulfilling my dreams, goals, plans and even relationships with others. But at least it became clear. It also dawned on me that, as a youngster, I was told that it was okay to be well versed at many things. I like to call it the "all-around syndrome." It is like being the "B" student, never excelling to one's full potential or developing true areas of expertise.

Uncovering your history will allow you to recognize the times when you might revert back to those old patterns. You will be better able to manage your life and business practices while opening up paths to greater potential. I do not want to discredit my past or yours. It can become one of your greatest assets for future decision-making. What we have all endured in our lives makes up our backbone, allowing us to discover and transform ourselves.

So, let me help you begin to discover your own behavior patterns by raising a few questions for you to ponder. Are you a person who gets things done? If so, you are already off to a great start. But maybe, like me, you begin tasks and then never complete them. Or, perhaps you make plans but just can't seem to get started. Do you "walk your talk" or are you often full of "you know what"? Do you try to do too many things (the all-around syndrome)? Are you organized or cluttered? Do you take responsibility for your actions or do you blame others? This is all important to know.

It is easy to read about how to change the direction of your life, but an entirely different story when it comes to actually taking action. That is why I want you to take 2 minutes to complete this simple exercise. If you are tempted to skip over it, you are likely a person who needs to work on getting things started. Begin the process of breaking that habit right now. Do not skip this exercise!

Directions: Write down where you currently are in your business (and in your personal life, if you wish), where you want to be, what you want to do, and what you hope to achieve and have for yourself in 5 and 10 years. Use extra paper, if necessary. You have **2 minutes only**. Go!

Where You Are Now

_____

_____

_____

Goals—5 Years from Now

_____

_____

_____

Goals—10 Years from Now

_____

_____

_____

Signature _____

Date _____

I gave you only 2 minutes so that you would not have time to stew over this and let an insecure mind control your decisions. It needed to come from your heart, what you really want, deep down inside. I hope that you thought big enough that when you accomplish your goals, you say, "Wow, I did that. I never thought I had it in me." If it makes you nervous to think about some of the things you will have to do to get there, then you are likely on the right track.

Now read your list to someone and tell them where you are going in the massage therapy profession in 5 years and 10 years. Can you do that? If not, ask yourself why. Listen to your resistance. Are you someone who is true to your word? You see, when you tell someone your plans, you are more inclined to carry them out. You have ownership of it and make a greater commitment to yourself. It resonates throughout your body, giving it meaning and reinforcing its importance.

Okay, you are about to embark on some unfamiliar territory. Your whole life, you have been conditioned to get only a certain amount done. For years, you have practiced the same habits over and over. It is now time for some reconditioning in order to maximize your massage therapy practice. How, you may ask? The initial vision you had for yourself is now your new energy source, the beginning of something new. The momentum for change begins with that vision. Unfortunately, for many, it also stops right there. What stops them? Who stops them? The answer is that they stop themselves.

It has happened to most of us. We can become weak, in a sense, and lose the warrior within ourselves. We must remember to do things for self-approval and not to seek that approval from others. Just think about how many times you did not do something because you were in fear of what someone would say or might think of you. You were afraid of how someone else would judge you. Do not let insecurity cause you to lose sight of your goals. Learn to overcome this.

Act On Your Vision

First and foremost, you have to embrace and believe in your vision. Have a relationship with it. LOVE it! Nurture it. Live your life as though your vision is already your reality. When you do this, you begin to break old inefficient habits and replace them with new, productive ones that actually help you achieve your goals and get there faster. We cannot change all old habits overnight, but we begin with one or just a few. It is a process of elimination and accumulation! This will gradually clean up the non-supportive elements in your life that are holding you back. This includes relationships that drag you down, tasks that are not good for you, lifestyles that work against you, etc. Create some new rules to live by. Do not start a new task until previous ones are complete. Make yourself accountable by implementing deadlines, check-off lists, and more to organize your day.

In fact, what does your current daily schedule look like? This is your life on paper. Record it and determine how much time is wasted so that you can find new ways to accomplish tasks to help you realize your goals. What would an ideal day look like to you? Create it and scrutinize it carefully. Is it attainable? If not, re-do it until you can make it happen. Then repeat this schedule over and over each day, week, and month. Consistency will keep you moving towards your goal. Here is an example of a schedule. Not all of the blocks are filled in, so be creative and fit it into your own life's structure.

Time	Sun.	Mon.	Tue.	Wed.	Thur	Fri	Sat.
6am		Workout					Extra Sleep
7am		Breakfast					Breakfast
8am		Work prep					Workout
9am		Work					Family/Social
10am		Work					Extra projects
11am		Work					Chores
12pm		Lunch					Lunch
1pm		Work prep					
2pm		Work					
3pm		Work					
4pm		Work					
5pm		Work					
6pm		Dinner					Dinner
7pm		Social family					
8pm		Extras					
9pm		Self					
10pm		Bedtime					Bedtime

Chapter Four Notes:

5

Why You Are

I have heard numerous reasons why some choose to become massage therapists. Among the most common are the ever-popular, "I want to be my own boss," or "I could make a killing as a therapist," or how about, "I want to help people," or "Massage feels so good, everyone should receive." These are all good motivations, indeed, although there could be a deeper reason for those thoughts.

Be Your Own Boss

"I want to be my own boss." Sure, that's for me. How about you? In our minds, we seem to have control when we are self-employed. We create each day the way we want it. This gives us a chance to truly live, but it can sometimes be difficult, especially for those who are used to being told how to conduct every aspect of their job including what time to get there, what clothes to wear, when to have lunch, how many breaks to take, vacations, who you work with, how much you can make, and the list goes on. It can be difficult to break out of that mold if you have spent years in this type of daily work environment. With so much control over all of this, it can be tempting to become relaxed and lose your discipline, focus, and concentration, particularly if you have been conditioned to the rat-race lifestyle of the corporate world.

To be a "boss" one must have the ability to problem-solve. As therapists, we are solving problems for our clients. We use soft tissue manipulation as our tool. For some therapists, this is not an easy task. It is a learned skill. In my opinion, if you can become good at problem-solving in one area, it can translate into other areas. It can be very rewarding to accumulate the knowledge and experience necessary to problem-solve, put your intentions into action, and be your own boss.

For those of you who need assistance to effectively be your own boss, I suggest that you create a checklist or to-do list and a plan of action that enables you to stay within your self-imposed deadlines. You can even do this with treatment protocols so that you do not accidentally miss critical steps. Hire your own business or life coach (which I have done). This is someone who you report to in order to keep your plans and goals organized and on track. He/she also provides problem solving support. It is well worth the cost, especially when you factor in how much could potentially be lost.

It does not take long for one to lose self-discipline. It is possible to wake up one day and wonder how you are going to pay the bills. This is most discouraging and will likely result in the choice to abandon the profession. The self-employed therapist needs to realize that problems are just part of life and there is no need to panic. You simply need to correct and move forward. Yes, this might be a bit harder than it sounds but, in reality, we already do this all day automatically. Things that seemed difficult to you years ago, you can now do without hesitation and without even thinking about it. Practice makes perfect, as they say. As we move through life, we constantly encounter new challenges. If you choose to avoid these challenges by following the exact same routine day after day, your growth will plateau. Once you get too comfortable, mediocrity can set in. Instilling a fear-based motivator (such as the ability to pay your bills) can actually be healthy for your business. It is a good fear to have as long as you can process it and deal with it. The more new problems and challenges you face, the better your overall potential as a self-employed therapist.

Sometimes, people want to be their own boss simply because they cannot get along with others. This can pose a problem. Ask yourself whether you would honestly hire yourself based on your personality and the work ethic you possess right now. If the answer is no or you do not know, I suggest you learn some people skills. They are a necessity in the massage therapy profession. This is a personal service business. Can you listen well to others? Do you usually correct people whenever they speak? Do you give your opinion on every subject of conversation? Do you have trouble admitting when you are wrong? As therapists, we have to listen and should only communicate our thoughts when asked. If this is a weakness for you, you must develop your interpersonal skills so that you are able to get along with others.

To avoid conflicts with clients, allow them to completely verbalize their thoughts. Then, confirm that you heard them by repeating back what they said. This communicates to your client that he or she has been heard and understood. You also avoid coming across as someone with a big ego, a "Mr. or Ms. Know-It-All." I have worked around many therapists who like to tell others how much they know. This only belittles the client and your business will suffer. Clients will only return to you if they like your work and if you have given them a sense of validation through your communication.

Making a Living as a Therapist

Making a lot of money depends on your definition of "a lot of money." There are more and more massage schools popping up these days. One of their marketing tactics is to claim that it is a very lucrative career. Often, they are even guilty of misleading students. For example, some will suggest that one can do 40 massages a week to yield such and such amount of dollars. Wrong, wrong, wrong! It does not work that way. Trust me. Money cannot be the primary lure. Before I address a massage therapist's income, let us take a look at a little bit of background.

The trend of more trained professionals entering the field could be nature's way of increasing the number of alternative practitioners, but maybe there is more to it than just nature alone. Given the massive problems within the health-care industry and the propensity to focus on the symptoms rather than the causes of illness, we have watched health problems escalate. The available options for dealing with health, wellness, aging, and longevity are currently very unbalanced. However, there does seem to be more awareness of and concern for global ecology. With this, more patients are seeking holistic solutions for their ailments. This demand is one reason for the growing number of holistic practitioners, and the increasing number of massage therapists is part of that greater movement. It is now one of the fastest growing professions. This change should be welcomed by all, particularly those who continue to suffer with pain, discomfort, and disease in their lives. Perhaps humans are discovering that many of the skills and answers to heal have actually been within us and amongst us all along. Too many have spent and are currently spending a small fortune on health coverage, prescription drugs, and other medical expenses, yet their conditions persist and even multiply.

As alternative health options continue to grow, it does not seem unreasonable for those just entering the industry to expect substantial financial gains. But current reality indicates otherwise. The National Occupational Employment and Wage Estimates have published that the annual national average is a mere $28,040 (2005) for the massage therapist. Although this figure could certainly change over the coming years, it explains much of the current drop-out rate. It is difficult to support oneself on that kind of income. One of my goals for writing this book is for you to have the inner tools to make 3 to 4 times that number or more. But it takes work, consistent work. Some people make a good living in this business because they have a formula that works for them. Chapters 7 and 8 of this book address some of those strategies.

For many therapists, like myself, there is a greater purpose. I genuinely love what I do and I see how it benefits people. But in addition to that, my desire is to provide for my family. If I don't, I could lose my house, car, assets, and more. Now that is a strong purpose. Fear is a motivator here. Have you ever noticed how we all tend to get motivated when our backs are against the wall? It never fails. That is when we get things done. Well, imagine if we used that same intensity in our practice every day. Wouldn't that create a great business? Actions that were once difficult to establish as part of our routine become easy due to repetition. In turn, new habits are formed.

Please keep in mind that being a massage therapist just for money minimizes the true nature of this profession. What is really happening is an exchange of energy. Yes, money is given as payment for your time. And it should be. But there is also great reward in the privilege of positively affecting someone you might not even know. Think about it. When someone comes to your office, they are putting a great deal of trust in you as a professional. Of all the people in this world, they have chosen you to help them. Furthermore, in order to do your job, you have to touch them. They are allowing you into their personal space. That level of trust is a privilege requiring your honor and respect. You must take this very seriously. In my experience as a therapist, it is obvious to me that most of those who remain in business for a long period of time understand this. On the other hand, it is not uncommon for those who have exited their careers early to never realize this.

And now *the* question: are you a therapist from your mind, body, or spirit? These are the "big three." They are all connected, but one is usually dominant given the situation. Have you ever noticed how you might think or react to something you have heard? Was it your mind, body, or spirit that guided your reaction? In my opinion, the massage therapy profession is a spiritual one in many ways. It is not mechanical, yet some businesses are run that way. It is disrespectful to treat human beings as though they are part of a herd of cattle, pushing them through a gate, one customer at a time. Typically, these businesses operate with no real meaning behind their offerings. It becomes all about the numbers and, at the core of it all, money; numbers in, versus numbers out. I acknowledge that we are seeing clients in exchange for a financial pay-off. But as you might recall, this type of healing has been around for many years, well before anyone seemed to notice the potential for a financial reward. This is a healing therapy that has persisted because it truly helps people and was a necessity for survival before modern day medicine emerged. I will reiterate that we must all be paid for our work, but feeling enthusiasm or a spirit for our work is a reward unto itself and it should not be depreciated.

Helping Others

I hope that a desire to help people is at least one reason you chose to be involved in this industry. So why did you or I have this desire to help others? The reason is likely different for each of us. When I was a very young child, my mother noticed what I would do around others who were sick or in pain. She said that I would run to their sides and promote well-being very quickly. My concern to help others was evidence of the dominance of my spirit's passion to assist those in need. I guess it stuck. The emotional satisfaction I felt for giving and helping felt good to me. I remember hanging out at the physical therapy clinic where my mother worked. I would just play with the gadgets and equipment while observing and listening in on rehab treatments first-hand. It was fun. I was in my element and my mind was focused on learning. I continue to feel that same enthusiasm for what I do today. It excites me to continue to learn new techniques and to teach others what I have learned.

For the most part, each one of us started our lives with massage when we were first born. Through touch, we felt secure, loved, healed, and pleased. And then, when and if we are lucky enough to become parents ourselves, we give the gift of touch and bonding in the same way to our own children as they enter the world. It is automatic, over and over throughout the generations. Nevertheless, we have, still today, a touch-deprived society. We are taught that adults (particularly men) must be tough and some believe that massage will soften you. It is not yet fully accepted as a standard form of treatment.

I still get odd reactions from people who are surprised by what I do for a living. It is strange how people can shut down when the topic is brought up. Some are interested and will ask questions while others will clam up and back off. The skeptics say there is no scientific evidence that it works, so why pay for it? Some think it is a waste of time or that it is just for the rich and famous. To them, massage is simply a luxury with no practical application. If you experience these reactions from people, decide to let it go. If you truly believe that the service you provide has value for people, this is a must.

To avoid becoming discouraged by those who do not yet accept your therapy services, always keep in mind that they are still potential clients. They are just not ready for it at this time in their lives. Not everyone is on the same page in life.

This individuality is what helps to make life interesting. Provide them with your information so that they can choose to contact you when and if the time is right. But, do not sit around and wait for them to do so. The lesson here is, just because we believe strongly that everyone should receive massage does not mean we should try to force or guilt someone into trying it. Be patient with others and respect their belief systems. It is critical that we not impose our opinions on them. This will only cause them to avoid you and prolong their healing process. They will try it when they are ready. Typically, this is after other traditional medical treatments have failed them. It could be years later when they pull your business card out of their desk drawer and decide to make an appointment.

Treating the Individual

To be the best at what you do, you must first enjoy it and, as alluded to before, be enthusiastic about it. I am talking about a genuine interest in your profession. Try to understand *why* you feel this way. For example, you may have experienced the therapeutic benefits yourself before ever becoming a practitioner. Massage therapy has helped me through some of the painful experiences that I have endured in my own life. Deep down, I do not want people to have to suffer with the same issues that I had. Since I was a recipient of massage therapy before I became a therapist, I thought that everyone should receive it. If I like it, then everyone else will like it too, thus it should be easy to have a great business. Quickly, I learned that this was simply not the case. Just because we like something does not mean that everyone else will.

You will connect with many people who have similar issues to those that you had, but they are not necessarily a carbon copy of your own. Sometimes as therapists, we can get caught up thinking that, because we have or had certain complaints, then so does everyone else. I see many passionate therapists try to persuade "newbies" (people who have never experienced massage) by schooling or grilling them so hard that they come across as confrontational or negative. This is not good for the therapist or the industry. In most cases, they are just really excited (spirit) about what they do, but they have not yet developed the skills to get clients on their table. Your own experience receiving massage was, quite possibly, your calling or awakening to become a healer, educator, and supporter. This healing gave you a passion and true understanding of the value of the therapy. You feel a sense of duty to deliver these benefits to others who seek your help. Like an inventor of a product, you want the world to know that it is available.

Your own story, the reason for your enthusiasm, needs to become a part of your unique niche. Consider making it a key aspect of your marketing.

We are all uniquely different in our structural, psychological, and energetic makeup. Those who deliver other forms of medical treatment often forget this and treat the human body as though it is so mechanical, even robotic. This "one size fits all" process is not a strategic solution in most cases. Treatments need to be more individualized. Have you ever had the chance to work with twins? They have so much in common beyond appearances, yet they can be so different. They, like others, require individualized treatments and, even if given identical forms of therapy, will not necessarily respond in the same way. You might also discover that one twin is more open to receiving massage than the other. If even identical twins can vary, then most certainly others do too.

Some people lacked that basic need for physical touch at a young age and are, therefore, uncomfortable with the idea of massage. On the other hand, others in the same situation might react by seeking massage in an attempt to fulfill this same need. To clarify, this need I am speaking of is not a sexual one. It is the basic need for human contact that begins the moment we are born. In fact, babies who do not bond with an individual in the early months of life are more likely to develop severe social problems.

The bottom line is that people come to us for various reasons. We deliver answers to questions, not so much verbally, but through the energetic transfer of touch. We can pass on our spirit (and receive theirs) when we come in contact with them. We might help them begin a new life, enable a chapter in their lives to open, or allow others to close.

Having raised the topic of human needs, it would be unfair not to address the flip-side of the issue. Do some massage therapists enter the profession because they lack something? For many, the ability to touch fulfills a need that they either did not get enough of as children or do not get enough of today. So looking at a deeper level, it is possible that some therapists provide others with their daily touch requirements while simultaneously meeting their own. This is definitely not always the case, but I raise the point in an effort to help you discover your own unique *why*.

Massage therapy is a mutual exchange of energy and support. There are reasons that clients seek your help and reasons why they might sometimes never return. Have you ever rubbed one the wrong way (pardon the pun)? Some clients stay with you for a certain amount of time and then choose to move on. It might be after just one visit, after many back-to-back visits, or there might be long gaps between visits. You could kill yourself trying to figure it all out. The reasons can be as varied as the individuals. Maybe it was just not the right fit and, in all likelihood, it will not be the last time it happens. Always keep in mind your *why*, focus on your passion for the profession, and continue to move forward.

Chapter Five Notes:

6

How You Are As a Therapist

How are you as a *professional* massage therapist? Let us take a look at the dictionary definition of the word, *professional*. This is a person who specializes in a field that is engaged in or suitable for a profession. The key words here are *specializes, engaged in,* and *suitable*. Think about those words and think about where you fit into each one of them. Do you specialize in something? Are you engaged in the profession? Are you suitable for the profession? The people who make the most money in this business are those who accomplish all three aspects of being a professional.

On a scale of 1-10, true professionals operate at a level of 10 on an almost daily basis. This simply means that they strive for the best from themselves. They always seek more education, emulate respected colleagues, take responsibility for their actions, and learn from their mistakes. Professionals are always the highest paid individuals in everything from sports to business leaders to respected community leaders. They push themselves a little bit more each day.

The Importance of Focus

To make more, you have to stretch yourself more. To get more, you have to do things differently than you have in the past. Professionals work to keep themselves from becoming distracted or upset by let-downs. They are problem-solvers focused on their mission. As therapists, we have to be focused on our business and our clients. We focus on our clients, of course, because that is the root of our business. Strong roots establish a strong business. If you are unfocused or inattentive to your clients, then your business will struggle. Focus affects you all the way down to the cellular level. It is the foundation of your habits from deep within. Your roots have to untangle in order to get rid of the bad stuff, i.e. your bad habits.

The simple definition of being focused is to be 100% present. This can be difficult to do. We all have to deal with information overload, emotional issues, and physical stress. One trick to maintain your focus is to ask yourself certain questions. This can help you remain focused during treatments and even throughout the day. It is so easy to get distracted by noises, comments from clients that are not really related to what you are doing, and your personal issues. When you get thrown off, the quality of your work will suffer.

Here are some questions to ask yourself during treatments:

1. What muscles am I releasing right now? Does my client know these muscles?

2. How are my body mechanics? Am I maintaining proper position? Is the client in the proper place and position on the table?

3. Is the client breathing properly? Am I breathing properly?

4. Can I improve my communication with the client? Can the client explain an issue differently so that I understand more clearly?

5. Does the client know what I am doing? Ask and tell.

6. What is the client feeling through energy releases?

7. What are my palpation skills telling me? What is the client sensing?

These are just a few examples, but notice that there is a two-way street here between the client and the therapist. They are interacting together; two minds, bodies, and spirits working together to meet a goal. This is double the power of intention, and it leads to better results. Most therapists who are professional, successful, and good at what they do, are aware of this interaction.

Specialize

A person usually becomes specialized within their profession by means of education and work experience. In this line of work, we can also specialize based on our own personal experiences. For example, at some point in your life, you may have suffered with Carpel Tunnel Syndrome. Perhaps you share some experiences with your client: jumping through the hoops of traditional medicine and going through the non-surgical routine, then finally receiving expert techniques that eliminated your CTS. These experiences become learned techniques that you use to help others who have been diagnosed with CTS. You become more specialized and you are of more value to clients with that condition. You have actually lived it and can, therefore, empathize with their situation.

The problem is that too many therapists remain generalized (meaning average), rather than become specialized. I often see therapists take CEU classes, intending to expand themselves, and then not use the skills that they spent their time and money to learn. They never even attempt to apply it. Why? It can be overwhelming to improve and become an expert in every area. Perhaps it is also the fear of doing something different with their clients. It is easier to stay within their comfort zone. The reality is that therapists cannot be experts in every area. To specialize means that you focus on just one or a select few.

This results in working at a level 5, on a scale of 1-10. When you work at a level 5, that is exactly what you will get: 5 pay, 5 life, 5 career satisfaction, etc. All of this will project on your clients. They can sense it. You become a mediocre therapist. In that range, there is boredom, and boredom is linked with depression. Working in this state can lead to unfulfilling experiences and an unfulfilling business. It is like stagnant water. You are not flowing. Get into flow by becoming specialized in an area.

The next step is to become more engaged in the profession. Let's return to my example of the therapist who specializes in Carpel Tunnel Syndrome. This therapist must engage in professional opportunities in order to become a leader in the specialty. This involves continuing education as well as teaching, speaking, writing books, and/or becoming a leader of support groups or clubs. All of this increases credibility and can result in more financial gain. Share your passion and do not get caught in the trap of doing the same thing over and over each week, month, or year of your life. This leads to mediocre levels, making it impossible to lead your field of interest. Eventually, you will be surpassed by others who continue to learn and develop themselves. Always search for more for yourself. This increases your value compared to other therapists.

Failure to grow and improve leaves the body, mind, and spirit in a state of "BLAH!" There is no stimulation and nothing is being fed to the soul. What happens when we confine ourselves to the same regime or box that we live in? We condition ourselves to stay there. Do you remember the biology experiment with the frogs in the jars? Ten frogs were put in jars without the lids so that they could jump out. Later, lids with holes to allow for air and food were placed on the jars. The frogs jump up against the lids for days. Soon after, they adapt and stop jumping. When the lids were later removed, the frogs did not attempt to jump out. They became accustomed to their environment and believed they could not get out. Or, the muscles were only conditioned to jump to the lid surface and down. They were trapped by their own belief system. Be careful of the box of belief systems that you have established.

Be Suitable for the Profession

To be suitable means to be appropriate for a given purpose. Who decides if you are suitable or not? You do. It is all about how you think and judge yourself. It is your business and your life, like a game with your mind. In sports, coaches have tryouts for teams or clubs. In business, management decides if you are a good fit for their corporation. But when you are in business for yourself, you decide if you are good enough. You decide if you can play or not. You decide if you can make the all-star team. So what are you going to be: a generalized practitioner or a true professional massage therapist? Either way is good enough for me because it is your life and business, not mine. I am not judging here. It is all about your personal goals and what you want to accomplish.

Have you ever met a professional athlete or CEO of a top firm who did not feel secure within the sport or business? They are strong from within and they know what they want. How you think of yourself is what makes you truly suitable or not.

Are you emotionally anchored down? You are if there is any doubt in your mind that you are suitable for any job. There will be a feeling throughout your body that is yielding fear or anxiety of some sort. This feeling is projected through your work. It is a negative energy that does not help in healing others. In our profession, it can wear you out to remain in this state too long.

During treatments, you should be giving positive energy that is stored and generated from you to the recipient (your client) that is ailing from pain or stress. If you are in a fear-based mode, there is no energy to be given or generated. It is like trying to jump-start a dead battery in a car with another battery that is too low. Low energy is unhealthy and can lead to illness within your mind, body, and spirit. It is also destructive for your business. In a healthy state, there is clarity and focus in what you do. Otherwise, you will lack motivation and will not be happy or satisfied with your work. You will always be looking for something else to do in an attempt to "find yourself."

A simple meditation exercise can be used to remove this anxiety or fear that is draining and limiting you as a therapist. While sitting in a comfortable position, close your eyes gently. Relax your entire body and breathe by inhaling all the way down into your belly. Repeat this breathing several times. Feel tensions releasing, letting go of the stresses of life. Be in the present moment, letting go more and more. Use this time to focus on yourself. It is time to think of the connection you have with yourself. Discover your inner self more and more within each breath. Allow your body to shift and be even more relaxed. When you are done, you should feel a sense of being grounded and at ease with your thoughts. Ask yourself if you are ready for work to continue. If not, repeat the process. You can be creative with this. Find what works best for you in order to experience a release.

Now, write down *how you are* as a professional massage therapist and what you can change to better yourself.

PART II
A Healthy Practice
and a
Healthy You

7

Get Clients Fast, Without Spending a Lot of Money

Let us now focus on how to get some clients fast. There are a number of methods, some more common than others. Many people like advertising, but as a general rule, I do not. In my experience, the expenses associated with traditional advertising in newspapers, magazines, or on the internet simply do not pay off.

There are, however, some exceptions. In a seasonal venue such as a ski resort with a limited local population, advertising might be necessary. If you are in this type of environment, be sure to take advantage of other, more cost effective approaches as well. You must work closely with staff members who come in contact with guests. For example, a hotel concierge can play a key role in getting visitors to you. Pay them a percentage of the business they refer to you or provide them with complimentary treatments. Make it worth their time to promote your services to guests. This will help ensure that they send business your way. Best of all, you will only pay them when you get paid (unlike advertising).

Word-of-Mouth Advertising

There is one form of advertising that I believe is the ideal way to build your client list. Best of all, it will not cost you a cent. It is called word-of-mouth advertising. One reason that it works so well is that it eliminates the greatest unknown for the client: the factor of customer satisfaction. No one wants to risk their precious time and hard-earned money, but when a person hears someone say that they had a great treatment from you, it gives your name and business credibility and reduces risk for that client. A typical media advertisement does not accomplish this.

In order to maximize your word-of-mouth advertising, implement a referral program within your business and make sure that all of your clients are aware of it. A win-win situation is always a good relationship builder. In my program, clients receive 1 free treatment for every 3 new clients they send in. This is an especially enticing incentive for those who have limited funds to pay for massage therapy but want the benefits. Be sure to also keep your eyes peeled for those clients who are natural salespeople and have the "gift of gab." Those who belong to clubs or groups can spread the word like "wildfire." Be creative and find what gives your particular client-base the strongest incentive to refer new clients. The key is to have others spread the word about your business and therapy. Just about everyone has internet access these days. E-mail is a great communication tool and most of your clients likely have e-mail lists of their own. Consider typing up a quick e-mail flyer to send to your clients. Ask them to forward your flyer to people they know who might be interested in your work. Include a discount as an extra incentive as well as a referral name so that your client will receive credit for your referral program. Try this and you will probably be surprised by how quickly word can spread. Your message can potentially reach so many people, all at no extra cost to you. Be sure to ask people to show up with the printed e-mail flyer so that you can track it. **(Important Note: Be sure to carefully consider your clients before doing this. Some might consider it spam and become offended. Know your clients well enough to determine who is open to receiving and circulating your promotional emails.)**

To build your business quickly, get your hands on as many people as possible (without burning yourself out, of course). I realize that it might be frustrating to hear that the way to build a client list is to get more clients. It can seem somewhat contradictory, but the truth is, you only need to start with a few people. That small number will snowball if you provide excellent service that truly helps them.

Bartering

Many therapists sit impatiently next to the phone, thinking that someone will call just because they have a listing in the phone book or an ad in the paper that offers a half-price treatment (I'll discuss ads and flyers in the next chapter). These therapists are clearly not aware of the power of the barter system. The barter system—use it! If you are just starting out, your goal is to get hands-on experience in order to spread the word about your services. **To get this experience, you must have others, not you, spread the word about you.** I cannot say this enough. The "You scratch my back, I'll scratch yours" approach works very well. There are countless partnership opportunities since we all have numerous expenses and already use the services of many other businesses. Here are just a few possible examples:

- rent for a place to work
- washing sheets
- massage supplies and business supplies
- maintenance of an office you might own
  (cleaning services, landscape services, handyman services)
- accounting
- computer technicians
- car mechanics
- physicians/chiropractors
- alternative health practitioners such as
  acupuncturists,
  nutritionists, other massage therapists
- personal trainers
- yoga instructors
- piano or guitar lessons
- dues for a health club

Be sure to consider any of your hobbies that might require supplies, coaching, or advice (triathlon, scrapbooking, photography, etc.). Be creative! Look for every opportunity to TOUCH SOMEONE. People need to experience your work in order to talk about it. In the past, I liked to do triathlons and running races, so I would bring my table to races. I would race and then set up my table. How convenient. I would meet so many people. I sometimes worked for free and sometimes charged for the service. You must check with the race directors to do this. Either way, they would experience a sample of my work and then book appointments at my office. All of these techniques have helped me build my own practice.

I have listed over 20 potential bartering partnerships for you. Do the math here. You have 20 people who are all in different walks of life socially, financially, educationally, etc. If these 20 people are satisfied with your treatments, and they are able to tell someone about you and speak from experience without the salesman approach, you can see how this can multiply quickly. There is really no money attached to it for you, only your time. I recommend trying to find one new professional to barter or trade with each week. Use your talents and services in exchange for theirs and promote them to your clients who express a need for a service such as theirs. Look at this list again. Many of these folks might need to build their client lists too. They will want to barter with you!

Another advantage of using the barter system is that, in the long run, it saves you a lot of time. On the list above, you are exchanging with individuals who are experts, or at least are better than you, at those particular tasks. Look at accounting, for example. It can take a long time for you to do your taxes. How about mowing your lawn? Do you have all of the necessary professional equipment to create curb appeal in a short amount of time? I am guessing that you probably do not. Saving this time allows you to establish more balance in your life so that you can pursue your hobbies, be social with family and friends, or take vacations. Time is a limited resource. Spend this time enjoying life. You have earned it.

Create "Partnerships"

Another type of person who can help you build your practice is the paying client who is in charge of a business with several employees. If you like doing chair massage gigs, then make sure you provide these clients with brochures about your chair massage services. They might hire you to come out to their business site. This is a great way to get more clients. Another reason that business owners or corporate executives make good clients is that they need their staff healthy and working. They want them to avoid complications such as neck and back pain, carpel tunnel, headaches, etc. This allows them to do their jobs better and more efficiently. You might be just the answer they were seeking in order to improve productivity. For this reason, they can also become fantastic gift certificate customers!

How else can you market without spending money? Create other partnerships with businesses and organizations that have a huge client base. Look at those that have the type of clients that you need. I use triathlon and running clubs, the YMCA and health clubs, and large business groups. I make presentations and conduct demonstrations to teach people about what I do and how it can benefit them. Presentations in such venues can generate instant credibility. You can give discounts, if needed, since you have not spent money on marketing to get those clients into your office. With the company or organization's permission, you can even sell things in the back of the room. Do not forget to get voluntary contact information from the attendees so that you can reach those who are interested in learning more about you. You might be surprised by the high rate of return (especially compared to pricey advertising and marketing).

Use the media for public relations opportunities. For example, I write short articles for magazines, newsletters, websites, newspapers, etc. Make sure these outlets target the clients you want. They need material. The key is to write in an article format, not a sales-pitch style. People often tune out ads. Articles, on the other hand, provide information and educate readers. You cannot beat the type of credibility that this free exposure can create when it is done on a regular basis. You will become recognized as an expert by many. People want to spend their time with, and money on, experts. If you have a great reputation, you will be successful. If you have no reputation, then how can you ever be successful?

Increase Value

Now that you have clients in your office, how do you get them to buy more of your services (back-end marketing)? I know that others have probably preached to you about selling items such as music, fancy lotions, candles, med creams, and self-massage tools that can make you a few extra dollars. This works fine for some additional income, but it can require upfront money which many therapists just starting out do not have.

I personally think the focus needs to be on bigger dollars by increasing your value to your client. To achieve this, you must have another separate service to offer them after the initial visit. In my business, I have two ways to attract clients. For some time, I have been a personal trainer and triathlon coach in conjunction with being a massage therapist. These two feed each other. When someone hires me to coach, my secondary sale is massage therapy. When someone hires me for massage therapy, my secondary service is coaching. Of course, not all of my massage clients are candidates for coaching, but since athletes are a group to whom I have marketed, they are good candidates often enough.

There are multiple combinations and approaches. Gain experience to be good at both. Find that other key niche. I recommend that it stays within the wellness industry. As you build your massage practice, listen to your clients and see what is in demand. They are always asking questions. That is how I became involved with personal training and coaching to begin with. I was constantly giving advice during a massage therapy session. It finally hit me, and I realized that I need to add this as a revenue source. So, I got certified as a triathlon coach. Here are a few examples of what you can do along with massage therapy in order to create that great one-two combo:

- Yoga
- Nutrition
- Meditation

- Acupuncture
- Massage Instruction
- Tai Chi
- Counseling
- Life Coach
- Dance Instruction
- Personal Trainer
- Colon Hydrotherapy
- Author

Now, you have DOUBLED your value to your client and the income potential from each client has also doubled. Their fear of time versus money is gone. The cost of marketing for the secondary service is zero. You cannot beat this. It is a win-win for both you and your clients.

All of the ideas in this chapter are commonly used by successful therapists. They will save you money and build up your client list quickly. The key is to apply them consistently.

Chapter Seven Notes:

8

Marketing Your Business Using Ads, Flyers, Brochures and Articles

Many massage therapists feel uncomfortable developing a marketing plan. It can feel like a foreign language you never learned. Indeed, it is a profession unto itself. Nevertheless, it needs to become part of the scope of your business (unless you have unlimited funds and can hire a marketing firm). As mentioned earlier, you cannot build a business by sitting next to the phone. Aside from the essential word-of-mouth advertising discussed earlier, there are other types of marketing to consider.

I am going to give you some quick and easy suggestions to help you create ads and flyers. Brochures are really just a longer version of the same thing, and articles are expanded versions of informational brochures. I have used all of these to get clients. Handing out flyers at road races and health fairs, distributing brochures at health fairs and other business lobbies, and writing articles for newsletters and magazines have all worked well for me.

Advertisements

Advertising can be such an enigma. There is never any way to know for sure which ads will be effective and which ones will become expensive mistakes. To increase your chances for success from this method of marketing, there are some points to consider when developing your ads.

Keep in mind that you only have a few brief seconds to catch readers' attention in order to maintain their interest in your message. Therefore, you must keep your language clear, concise, and stimulating. At the same time, establish what makes you unique and special. Define why someone should come to you instead of some-one else. Make your ad convey *who you are* to the reader (Chapter 1).

Words are critically important. The mind receives the words that are read or heard and then relays a feeling to the body. When people feel good about what they hear or read, they will buy the product or service, or at least want more information. Keep this in mind when you develop an ad, flyer, or brochure. To get people into your office the fastest, make this connection.

Use only crystal clear communication in your message that leaves no room for confusion. Practice writing ads that will grab readers' attention within a couple of seconds and will hold their attention for about 30 seconds longer. If your message lacks clarity, the customer will be "lost" and choose not to even dwell on your ad, much less call or book an appointment. In the massage therapy industry, one of the key differences between successful and unsuccessful marketing is the clarity of the message. To be clear is powerful. It is an essential skill that will develop with practice. You'll need to do some test runs with different words and phrases to see what works for your uniquely special business and in your area.

The key words here are *uniquely special business*. Write in a way that educates the public about you and explains why they need to come to you instead of others. Show the value of your service so that people will be willing to drive farther, if necessary, or even pay a higher rate in order to see you.

For example, if you market a simple message telling people that you are a massage therapist and charge a certain rate, this only gives them minimal information about you and what they will get for their time and money. However, when you include that you are a therapist with 15 years of experience and have helped many people in pain from traumatic and repetitive use injuries, you tell potential clients something special about you. Be sure to conclude the message with an action statement that encourages them to contact you for more information or to visit a website.

Flyers

To begin a flyer, you need to address a few things:

1. Who you are—your position and credentials (to give credibility)

2. Who you are catering to (what type of client)

3. The problem(s) you solve

4. What makes you unique

5. Make people take action with the information you give them.

If you don't have all five of these within the message, your chance for success is very limited.

Wouldn't it be great to be able to attract more people with a few simple words? That is exactly what good advertising, done properly, accomplishes. Use words that sell and keep people's interest. In the wellness business, there is a short list of words and key phrases that can work over and over. We have to avoid objections. Pain and pleasure are what drive our business, so they have to be addressed from the start and within only a few seconds.

For example:

Imagine Life Without PAIN!

Greg Spindler, LMT, CSET, is a certified Structural Energetic Therapist® who specializes in relieving acute and chronic pain. He is the only SET therapist in South Carolina.

For more information and testimonials on how this therapy can help you get out of pain the fastest, please call **1-888-SET-2001** or visit **www.gregspindler.com**.

A flyer will usually take up a whole page. In this example, you can see that I have provoked thought with the word *imagine* and a feeling with the word *pain*. This headline hooks the reader quickly. Your headline should be larger and/or in bold-face type.

I then clarified that I do specialized work that focuses on people in pain. Use of the word *certified* and the abbreviated endorsements *LMT* and *CSET* behind my name all establish credibility. They show that I am an expert.

Using the word *only* makes me unique too. The word *only* helps to create the unique special value that I mentioned earlier. It should be included quite often in your marketing. I also used the word *fastest*. Words that end with—*est* are great attention-getters. Examples of other—*est* words are *wealthiest, quickest, slowest, happiest, busiest, longest, shortest, strongest,* and *weakest*. They all have the power to grab the attention of your audience. Key words like these should be used throughout.

The contact information, including phone number and website, is displayed last and is the reader's call to action. Make it stand out using color, boldface type, or a larger font.

Brochures

Starting with the example flyer, we can now build an entire brochure. Expand on the following:

1. Give more information about Greg Spindler (a bio)

2. Specify what types of pain can be relieved with this therapy: back pain, neck pain, carpel tunnel, etc.

3. Define SET; give a description of SET in better detail

4. Provide testimonials from some of the people who have been helped by SET. Testimonials may or may not add credibility, but, more importantly, they give the readers something and someone with whom they can identify. It is the next best thing to calling the readers by name. Those who share some elements of the testimonials will relate to the stories.

5. Include the location address and office hours.

Articles

People are typically more likely to read articles than ads. They tend to make a more legitimate impression. An article would include all of the same expansion as above, but would provide an even more expanded version of the solutions to their problems (in this example, pain). Educate readers by explaining specifically what you do and how you help people when they come to see you. This helps to establish you as an expert. Remember, experts get the most business.

You might also choose to write your article in an interview format. Write your own questions (keeping your customers in mind) and answer them. You often see this on websites' *Frequently Asked Questions* pages. This can help potential clients make an informed decision. I suggest writing one of these up and send it to a newspaper or magazine in your local area as a press release.

You have to be willing to practice in order to get good at marketing. As mentioned earlier, it possesses a degree of mystery that requires trial and error. It is an ongoing process. Do not expect perfection on your first try. However, your writings, both short and long, have the potential to radically increase your business. Focus on offering solutions to problems for your potential clients.

Chapter Eight Notes:

9

Wellness, Simplified

Disclaimer statement ... The information in this chapter is solely for educational purposes. It is not intended as medical advice nor is it a substitute for appropriate healthcare and treatment. If you have an illness, please consult a licensed healthcare practitioner.

Anyone who thinks that being a massage therapist is not a strain on the human body is CRAZY! Well, maybe not crazy. They just do not understand. When I entered the business, I thought I was in shape and could handle anything. Well, I became schooled on that thought very quickly. Good body mechanics is important, but it is not enough. You must also be healthy and follow a wellness plan.

Physical Limitations and Body Mechanics

I often observe therapists at work or in seminars and workshops, Unfortunately, I continually see the same "don'ts" that are stressed at most schools and in massage therapy books. I see therapists bending their backs too much as they lean across tables, have table heights too high, have flexed or extended wrists, extended thumbs, and the list goes on. Their egos say they're indestructible; that is, until injury sets in and they realize they are human and vulnerable too. They lose their income and sometimes are forced out of the profession. Awareness and prevention such as exercises and stretches will help to keep you going. You may have heard the saying, "People take better care of their cars than their bodies." Do not fall into this costly trap.

Repetitive use injuries like carpel tunnel and tendonitis are among the leading health reasons why therapists leave the profession. These issues usually result from taking on too much work too fast and failure to schedule rest days. Some therapists overbook themselves or work in a facility that demands more than safe and appropriate amounts of work. The human body needs to build up clientele slowly to enable the body to develop the strength necessary to carry the load.

Our bodies are not just limited to repetitive use injuries like carpel tunnel syndrome. We are at risk for a host of other injuries as well as strains in major muscle groups. We sometimes lift heavy legs and apply pressure that puts torque on our bodies. If you offer outcalls, you carry tables up and down stairs or across bad weather like snow or ice. It can deliver a blow to your business if you are taken out by an injury.

In the world of endurance sports, the recommended time to build a base is 10% each week. That same rule should apply when building a massage therapy practice. Consider yourself an athlete when you are doing massage. You are building up your muscle groups to be able to handle more of a load within a specific period of time. Therefore, following the 10% rule can keep you under control and out of trouble.

Body awareness skills are helpful in recognizing signs of injury before they happen. Be your own consultant. Your body speaks to you with subtle changes as well as more obvious problems to warn you that trouble could be on the way. The most effective way to develop body awareness is to receive massage therapy yourself. Practice what you preach and mark it on your calendar on a weekly or bi-weekly basis. It must be a part of your life and routine. Visit a therapist who pays proper attention to potential trouble sites. This will give you a sense of awareness so that you can make assessments and change your daily activities as needed.

Another way is to do simple stretching exercises on each body part that you use during your massage work. Use a head-to-toe checklist and ask yourself what your body needs each day. For example, flex and extend your wrists to check for pain, adequate flexibility, and strength in each direction.

Are you losing flexibility over time? Are you gaining weight? Become educated and in tune with your body. Consider taking yoga or Pilates classes to further increase your body awareness. All of these will make you a better health practitioner who is able to recognize similar conditions in others.

Save your hands and save your body. It is your tool of your trade. If you were a truck driver, you would not dream of ruining or running down your truck. If you were in construction, you would not do the job with poor, ineffective tools. If you were a fisherman, you would make sure you have adequate gear and tackle to catch fish. Do not underestimate what you, the therapist, go through day after day. The inevitable consequence of that is pain within your own body, ironically the very condition you are working to alleviate in others. I estimate that 10-20%

of my clients are massage therapists, physical therapists, or occupational therapists. They, too, continue to make the same mistakes over and over, but by seeking massage therapy, they lessen their chances for injury.

Altering one's lifestyle in order to keep up with business is a challenge. It is human nature to resist change. But if you **truly** desire the rewards of change, the task is much less difficult. There are plenty of books, courses, seminars, and classes available to help you with illness and injury prevention, exercise, and wellness. For the successful therapist, it is good to have the knowledge not only to help yourself, but also to know what exercise programs your clients engage in. Stay current with trends. Be open-minded to things that are new and check them out. Become a member at a facility to help you explore the evolution within the fitness industry.

Here are a few books to consider:

Strengthening:
Core Performance by Mark Verstagen
The Weightless Workout by Jerry Robinson

Self Treatment:
Save your Hands by Lauriann Greene
The Pain-free Triathlete by Julie Donnelly

Flexibility:
Yoga for Athletes by Aladar Kogler
Active Isolated Stretching by Aaron Mattes

Since the "massage athlete" is active all day long, it is neither necessary nor a good idea to work out intensely as you might see others do. The purpose of your exercise program is for stimulation and to awaken the body to prepare it for more work throughout the day. This suggests that morning exercise is more beneficial to the body than evening workouts when the body is preparing to wind down. It only takes 30-60 minutes a day, 6 times a week. One day should be a total rest day. Make it a part of your daily routine by scheduling it in just as you would a business appointment. In many ways, it is a business appointment. Your business depends on your good health. In my opinion, you should focus on aerobic exercise 3-4 days (with the most time duration), and flexibility or strength training the rest of the week.

Note how you hold yourself around the massage table. As you learned in school, your body mechanics are important. However, your instructors likely did not point out the weaker areas of your body. Over time, we pick up bad habits that initiate imbalances that create more dominant sides, especially within those weaker areas. An example would be the lunge position being stronger on one side of the table than the other. Take the time to go through your stances and the mechanics involved in order to identify your weaker areas. Then do exercises to help strengthen them and create flexibility. My next book will address in greater detail which specific areas are commonly weak for therapists and how to strengthen them.

A Wellness Plan

Teaching and participating in workshops enables me to see the strong and the weak within this profession. So many therapists have the skills and knowledge to do very well with a practice. Some of them are just missing the last ingredient to help them along each day, week, month and year to come. These are therapists who do not lead a lifestyle which supports a massage therapy practice. Your wellness must be viewed as a requirement in your life, just like a professional athlete. It is critical to take care of the body's needs, day in and day out. The modern massage therapist needs to understand this as a way of life.

Some therapists become so busy taking care of clients that they do not make time for their own care. That is like having an overweight cardiologist who is supposed to possess a greater knowledge about health. What example does this give the client? I continually see therapists who smoke, are overweight, are weak in structural balance, stay up too late, are never rested, have alcohol/drug consumption issues and/or poor, poor diets. People can become so consumed with their addictions that they actually forget what feeling good is like. They begin to lose the ability to recognize when they do not feel quite right because they simply cannot remember how that feels. These folks cannot truly take care of others when they will not take care of themselves. They will likely end their massage careers early. That is the long-term consequence of poor choices.

There is a disturbing pattern with the typical rat-raced American lifestyle. Work, work, work until you get ill. Recover. Work, work, work until you get injured. Recover. It repeats over and over again. Eventually, you may not fully recover. You then have a handicap. You might not even realize that this handicap could develop into a disease or dis-ease. It is a shame how we entered into this world so pure and clean, only to trash ourselves. YOUR BODY IS YOUR NUMBER ONE INVESTMENT IN LIFE! TAKE CARE OF IT!

My experiences as a successful massage therapist, personal trainer, triathlon coach, and competitive athlete, have all enabled me to observe and personally experience what actions help one become a healthy massage therapist as well as what habits stand in the way. You might be surprised by how simple it can be to become healthier than you are right now in just 30 days. In our fast-paced society, we cannot be perfect, but we can make choices that greatly benefit us. We are inundated with an overwhelming number of fad diets, workouts, gimmicks and opinions on this topic. We seem to cycle through them all over and over. Who is right and who is wrong? It all becomes so confusing. But good health is achievable. The solution is to stick with some basics and be consistent. This means no more harmful diets, just lifestyle changes that promote lifelong wellness.

Your day is not composed of a series of isolated events. Each part of it supports and affects other parts of the day. There are reasons why we get up when we do, eat when we do, work when we do, and relax when we do. When in proper balance, it is a cycle in continuous flow. Placing stress on one or more parts of the cycle breaks down health, causing illness. Following a period of rest, the body will typically recover, allowing the person an opportunity to start over with better habits. Unfortunately, the lessons of illness are often short-lived. People tend to forget how their choices impacted their health (or they never realized the connection in the first place). The habits of overstressing one or more areas of the cycle eventually cause illness to return.

Although we are all different, the body's basic design is the same for all. There is an ideal schedule that the human body is meant to maintain. The closer you live to the schedule your body is intended to follow, the better your results. I have witnessed many positive changes in people's lives, wellness, energy, athletic performances, emotional states, and even creative breakthroughs. I am going to present a 24-hour timeline for you to compare with your current life schedule. In all likelihood, you will find discrepancies between this timeline and your own life. It is a great starting point to achieve improvement in your health.

When I coach clients, I begin by learning their sleep and rest cycles. Without that information, training programs cannot work. It is the most important controllable aspect of successful training. Bedtime for an adult should ideally be at 10:00 p.m. It is when the body wants to shut down to recover and begin replenishing from the day of work (living). There is no such thing as "catching up on sleep." The body has certain jobs to do during those nighttime hours. You should be at rest for 7-8 hours. In reality, the body is not really resting at this time. It is a productive part of the cycle when the body is hard at work for you to have energy, alertness, and the ability to function the next day. During the day as a "massage athlete," you have stressed your body. During the nighttime period, growth hormones are released to repair and renew your cellular system. If you miss this rejuvenating period due to being up late or remaining active, improper or insufficient amounts of hormones are released into the body, leading to premature aging. The term "beauty sleep" is certainly an accurate one.

One of the most powerful organs in the body, the liver, is hard at work too. It has the job of producing bile for digestion, detoxifying the body, and a host of other functions too long to list. The liver needs the body to remain at ease (sleep) in order to get this job done. Otherwise, the body will be unable to detoxify, balance chemically, and will not have enough bile for proper digestion the following day. If these functions do not occur in the body, even for a short period of time, results include weight gain, chronic fatigue, and even cancer. You must get adequate sleep at the proper time of day. The body relies on the secretions of stress hormones to stay awake or to stay active. Once these become depleted, the body shuts down from over-fatigue. When this happens, many turn to alternative forms of energy including caffeine from coffee and sodas, cigarettes, sugar, etc. in order to keep going. This escalates into an even more stressed body with foul nutrition sources.

As the early morning hours approach (after 3:00 a.m.), the body must prepare for the elimination of wastes stored in our bodies. Fecal matter is formed for bowel movement and urine from the kidneys is generated and sent to the bladder for urination upon awakening. Even our skin eliminates toxins on the surface, giving us the desire to shower in the morning upon awakening. I like to help the skin and lungs with a workout in the morning to flush more through perspiration. Our lungs expel more than half of the toxicity in our bodies. A simple walk or jog 3-4 times per week helps to bring up the trapped toxicity deep within the lung tissues. If aerobic exercise is not your style, deep breathing exercises are also effective.

A breakfast around 7:00 or 8:00 a.m. is best for many. Breakfast might be the most important meal of the day, but do not confuse this to believe that it should be the largest. Our bodies are working slower at this time, so eating a heavy meal is taxing to the system. Your morning is now ready to be filled with great mental tasks and other projects. The hours of 8:00 a.m.–12:00 noon are productive ones, nourished from proper sleep, nutrition, and stimulation of exercise. At this time, begin consuming your daily intake of fresh clean water. Keep a bottle or glass nearby to remind you of this critical duty. Water is the lubricating source for everything in the body.

Between the hours of noon and 2:00 p.m., the body wants and needs nutrition. Be certain to consume healthy foods since the body now has a majority of the digestive juices waiting for you to eat your largest meal of the day. Note how other countries allow for this as many of them routinely close up shops and businesses for that very reason. Now is the time for raw vegetables and fruits since our bodies have the appropriate amount of digestive juices for the task. It is important that we respect the body's cycle and give it what it needs.

Continue your water intake throughout the afternoon work hours in order to maintain correct hydration levels before dinner between 6:00–8:00 p.m. Most people make the mistake of over-consuming dinner and eating past 8:00 p.m. Dinner should be the second largest meal of the day. After that hour, the body needs time to unwind. The release of melatonin begins to encourage us to be in bed by 10:00 p.m. I encourage therapists not to take clients so late that they are unable to do this.

We live in a society of 'hurry up and get things done.' During these pressing time schedules, I see many people, therapists included, who succumb to fast food or junk food consumption just to keep up with their daily activities. All too often, people use microwave ovens to cook or heat up food in order to save time. Although it is rarely publicized, it is well documented what microwaves do to food. They basically destroy the nutritional value of even the healthiest foods, turning them into junk. They become merely waste products. Massage therapists must understand why they eat, when they eat, and how they eat. How can a toxic therapist provide quality work or have a positive energy exchange? Food for thought: Could a toxic body actually create a toxic mind and spirit?

In order to have the ability to work each day with a positive energy flow to your clients, you must consistently eat nutritious foods. Stay away from processed foods as much as possible. The chemicals that are used in such foods wreck the immune system and create an energy system that is suppressed to its lowest level.

Drink plenty of clean water for hydration and cellular flushing. Using kinesiology, you can test someone for adequate hydration. Asking one to hold there right arm out in front of them with palm down, test for strength by asking client to resist the therapist's downward pressure. Then give a slight pull on a hair of the scalp while testing the outstretched arm for resistance. If the arm goes weak, then the client is dehydrated. If strong, he/she is adequately hydrated at that time. Begin and end each day with a glass of water. Sleeping while dehydrated strains the working organs, preventing their efficient operation. But be careful not to over-consume liquids with each meal. We live in a "big gulp" society and many people are simply unaware of the proper times to hydrate. Drinking too much during a meal dilutes the digestive juices and prevents proper digestion. A good nutritional opportunity goes to waste and the problem only worsens when one chooses to drink a sugary beverage. It is no wonder we have such a high obesity rate. Whenever you put something in your mouth, ask yourself, "Is this helping me or hurting me?" It is a choice.

In conclusion, it is important to give the body what it needs, especially given your physical job as a therapist. Proper rest, stimulation, and nutrition allow the body to deliver to the mind and the mind to respond to the body. My purpose here is not to be preachy. We are all human and we do not make perfect choices 100 percent of the time. Do not kick yourself when you stray from the ideal diet and schedule. Remember that it is an accumulation of small lifestyle changes that can make the big difference in your health and wellness. As you make these changes, you will likely feel compelled to include more positive changes down the road. Eventually, a healthier lifestyle will become your new habit. Spirit then flows in the direction of growth for a harmonious life.

Chapter Nine Notes:

About the Author

Greg Spindler is a nationally certified licensed massage therapist as well as a certified Structural Energetic Therapy® (SET) therapist. He is a member of both the American Massage Therapy Association and the Florida State Massage Therapy Association.

Like most massage therapists, Greg started his practice on a shoestring budget. He learned from his own process of trial and error in real world experiences. This has allowed him to prosper at an elite level of the business, fully supporting his wife and two young boys. He is actively involved in the expansion and growth of the massage therapy profession. He is an assistant instructor to Don McCann (founder of SET), a published author, and has appeared on local radio shows.

His interest in the profession developed from his background as an athlete. He is a nine-time Ironman finisher, a certified personal trainer, a triathlon coach, and a repeated USAT All-American. Greg competed in the Ironman World Championship in Hawaii in 1994 and 1996, one such qualification resulting from a sub 2-hour Olympic distance triathlon (1996). In addition, he has completed Boston, Atlanta, and Disney marathons. Before he could help others, he first had to help himself. Struggling through his own injuries and the resulting setbacks, he learned the causes of injury as well as effective methods of treatment.

Greg continues to be involved in the sport and passes his experience and in-depth training knowledge on to others as a triathlon coach and a running coach. He believes it is important to create workouts and realistic goals on an individual basis. Developing strong skills in runners and triathletes cannot be approached universally due to the number of variables unique in each individual. As a natural motivator and hands-on teacher, Greg provides his clients with personal attention to help them become their best. He also teaches body awareness and mental strength which are keys to athletic excellence.

Greg's mission is to expand each individual's potential whether in the massage therapy profession, athletics, personal growth, or overall wellness for a better quality of life. He wants you to achieve your goals!

978-0-595-47946-7
0-595-47946-4

Printed in the United States
103283LV00005B/619-666/P